MESSIAEN

Oxford Studies of Composers

Oxford Studies of Composers (13)

MESSIAEN

ROGER NICHOLS

London

OXFORD UNIVERSITY PRESS

NEW YORK   TORONTO

1975

Oxford University Press, Ely House, London W. 1

GLASGOW   NEW YORK   TORONTO   MELBOURNE   WELLINGTON
CAPE TOWN   IBADAN   NAIROBI   DAR ES SALAAM   LUSAKA   ADDIS ABABA
DELHI   BOMBAY   CALCUTTA   MADRAS   KARACHI   LAHORE   DACCA
KUALA LUMPUR   SINGAPORE   HONG KONG   TOKYO

© Roger Nichols 1975

ISBN 0 19 315428 5

Grateful acknowledgements are due to the following publishers for permission to reproduce music examples: Durand, Paris (exx. 3, 4, 5, 13, 16, 17, 18, 19, 20, 21, 22, 23, 25, 26, 27, 28, 33); Leduc, Paris (exx. 1, 2, 6, 7, 8, 9, 10, 11, 12, 14, 15, 24, 29, 30, 31, 32, 35, 36, 37, 38, 39, 40, 41, 42, 43, 44, 45); Universal Edition (London) Ltd. (ex. 34).

PRINTED IN GREAT BRITAIN
BY W & J MACKAY LIMITED
CHATHAM

CONTENTS

753702

INTRODUCTION

OLIVIER Messiaen was born on 10 December 1908 at Avignon. That is what the history books say and in a way they are correct. Yet, from the point of view of art, Olivier Messiaen was 'born' before the day of his birth, when his mother, the poetess Cécile Sauvage, wrote a series of poems for the son that she was carrying—that he was a son she had no doubt:

Enfant, pâle embryon, toi qui dors dans les eaux,
Comme un petit dieu mort dans un cerceuil de verre,
Tu goûtes maintenant l'existence legère
Du poisson qui somnole au-dessous des roseaux.

The musicality of this, the opening verse of one of the poems of *L'Âme en bourgeon*, suggests that the child of such a mother might well be no ordinary talent. Messiaen's father was an English teacher and scholar, best known for his translations of the complete works of Shakespeare. From him, Messiaen acquired a love of Shakespeare's plays, which he declaimed vigorously and at length; from his mother a love of poetry and of fairy stories. His father and uncle were called up to the war and in the company only of his mother and grandmother he devoted himself to reading and to putting on puppet plays—Shakespeare, Calderón, Goethe. . . .

His taste for music was awakened a little later, by the scores of the *Damnation of Faust* and *Don Giovanni*, given to him as Christmas presents in 1916. Two years later, the Messiaens moved to Nantes and here the young Olivier was taught harmony by Jehan de Gibon. Most important of all, this teacher gave his 10-year-old pupil the score of Debussy's *Pelléas et Mélisande*; in Messiaen's own words 'a real bombshell . . . probably the most decisive influence of my life'. In 1919 his father's appointment to a post at Grenoble brought the family to the mountains which today remain for the composer a primary source of inspiration. In the same year Messiaen entered the Paris Conservatoire, from which point his education may be said to have followed more normal paths, with the proviso that while walking those paths he had eyes for more than the traditional check-points. In the years 1926-9 he won 5 first prizes but still had the time to apply himself to the study of Hindu rhythms, Greek modes, and plainsong.

Lastly, or rather firstly, through all these influences and activities, one central thread runs unbroken. 'I have the good fortune,' says Messiaen, 'to be a Catholic; I was born a believer . . . A number of my works are dedicated to shedding light on the theological truths of the Catholic faith. That is the most important aspect of my music . . . perhaps the only one I shall not be ashamed of in the hour of death.'

1926–1934

H<small>E</small> had been composing music since the middle of the First World War. In 1929 he failed the preliminary exam for the Prix de Rome. In 1930 he passed the preliminary but failed to win the prize with his cantata *La Mer*. Clearly, he was a man to watch. But there was no 'affaire Messiaen' as there had been an 'affaire Ravel' 25 years earlier. The only works of his in print at this time were *Le Banquet céleste* (1926) for organ and the eight piano Préludes, published in 1929 on the insistence of Messiaen's composition teacher, Paul Dukas.

It is tempting to describe *Le Banquet céleste* as a small work. On paper so it is, just 25 bars long. But at the speed prescribed by the composer it lasts some 6 minutes and, more important, the effect on the listener is far from small. How is this achieved? Partly by the sheer slowness of it. In the first edition, Messiaen gave no metronome mark and wrote the piece in $\frac{3}{4}$ time; in the second edition of 1960 he doubled the note-values and gave a metronome mark because organists were playing it too fast (Ex. 1). At this speed the piece is decidedly taxing for

Ex. 1

R. voix celeste, gambe, bourdon 8'
P. flûte 4', nazard 2⅔', doublette 2', piccolo 1'
G. R.G. | Péd. tir. P. seule

the player: for example the first chord should last for 7 seconds, and yet he must keep some sense of continuity from chord to chord. Some critics might argue that each chord is a sound-event and needs only to be appreciated as such, but this is to fly in the face of the music. What Messiaen has done, at the age of 17, is more radical still: he forces us to rethink our notion of time, so that we hear the logic of harmony and melody but without feeling ourselves tied to a mundane beat. The harmony itself is not difficult to follow, but it too has individuality. Bars 1–8 are based on the flux between dominant and tonic, although a pure dominant 7th is not heard until bar 20. The pure tonic is reached already in bar 8 but, far from being a resting-place, it serves more as a launching-pad from which the next 2 bars lift off. The harmony of bars 8 and 9 is largely responsible for this increase in tension and deserves careful study.

The chromaticism of the first 7 bars is clearly controlled by the bass of each bar. In bar 8 Messiaen develops the harmonic implications of the first bar, based on what he has called 'modes of limited transposition'. The usual procedure, indeed Messiaen's own, is first to produce a list of the modes and then of the harmonies derived from them, but at the same time he is insistent that the harmonies came first, as manifestations of musical colour, and only later did he tabulate these harmonies and relate them to a mathematical system. Mode I is the whole-tone scale, which he uses sparingly. Bar 8 of Ex. 1 is built on harmonies of Mode II (Ex. 2).

Ex. 2

This mode can be transposed through 2 semitones but after that it returns merely to a different order of the original notes. It is Messiaen's favourite mode throughout the 1930s and pervades much of *Le Banquet céleste*, but in bar 9 the language returns to the usage of Debussy in its parallel triads. After the modal atmosphere of the previous bar these triads are like an invigorating injection and their effect lasts, through the return of modal harmony, up to the decorated reprise of the opening.

Formally, the piece can be classed as AA'Coda. In other words *Le Banquet céleste* is not about themes, contrasts, or the dramatic inter-play of motifs, but about the establishment and prolongation of an atmosphere, in which different ideas are heard but to which they are always subservient. The chromatic modes (to give them a less precise but more convenient title) are Messiaen's prime means of creating such an atmosphere. Within it, pedal notes can be added, stops drawn and cancelled without violence to the musical sense. The coda is in no way a summary of experiences undergone, merely a leisurely settling on to the dominant 7th that was promised by the opening chord.

The systematic alternation of chromatic modes with more conven-tional tonal ideas, seen in bars 8 and 9 of Ex. 1, was something that Messiaen was to pursue for a time. He declared himself particularly attracted by the 'charm of impossibilities' that the modes possessed, and he may well gain a kind of mathematical satisfaction from their limitations. But there are dangers, and it seems that he recognized them from the first. For the ordinary listener, the limitations are not so much mathematical as aesthetic: he can recognize the modes easily enough after a little experience, and may just as easily tire of them if their atmosphere is to be the whole substance.

In the Préludes for piano Messiaen's debt to Debussy is fully paid, but, as the composer has been moved to insist, there is plenty of Messiaen as well. In attributing these pieces too wholeheartedly to Debussy's influence critics have pardonably been misled by titles like 'Les sons impalpables du rêve' and 'Un reflet dans le vent', which are almost an impediment to real listening. In 'Les sons impalpables' (Ex. 3) Messiaen for the first time combines two chromatic modes, II

Ex.3(a)

(cuivrez la partie supérieure)

Ex.3(b)

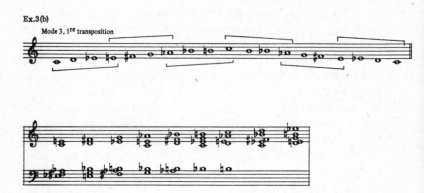

Mode 3, 1ʳᵉ transposition

in the left hand with III in the right. The transpositions of the modes are carefully chosen so that the two hands have 6 notes in common, 4 of which make up the first chord in the left hand part and keep the whole of this example close to the basic A major tonality. The ostinato of the right hand looks forward, in its simple way, to things to come and at the same time is interesting in its own right for the manner in which the melodic curve is constructed. The downward arc is built of 3 groups, decreasing in length from 4 notes to 3 notes to 2 notes. The acceleration in the descent provides the driving power behind the ostinato and the tension-raising asymmetry is balanced by the tension-releasing symmetry of the answering upward curve. The polarity between symmetry and asymmetry is, as we shall see, one of Messiaen's constant preoccupations, one that he explores at a great variety of levels. The ostinato returns three times in the course of the piece, always in combination with the left hand melody. At its last appearance the ostinato first goes its own way and is then followed by a version of the left hand melody (Ex. 4). The listener's attention, so far focused on the two ideas as an entity, is now directed to them separately, an unorthodox but perfectly logical and satisfactory way of signalling that the end is at hand.

Ex. 4

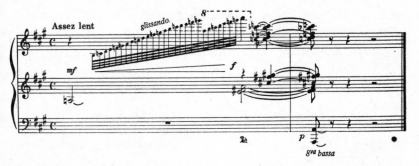

The final 9-note chord may possibly be analysed as some kind of synthesis of the two chromatic modes used in the piece, but it is probably just a very personal version of a triad on A, touched by an evocative ambiguity between major and minor. Messiaen certainly takes beautiful advantage of the construction of the piano in the timing and placing of the low octave A. 'Sons impalpables' indeed.

What the construction of the piano will not allow is the kind of temporal dislocation brought about in *Le Banquet céleste*. For that the organ is the perfect instrument, approached in perfection only by the string orchestra. Interestingly enough, Messiaen's first orchestral work to be performed in public returns to this attack on time and on man's conservative notions of it. *Les Offrandes oubliées* (1930) is a triptych representing successively the Cross, man's descent into Sin, and the promise of salvation offered by the Eucharist. This ternary form naturally involves Messiaen in establishing contrasted atmospheres within a single work. In the *Diptyque* for organ (1930) he had faced the same problem and had simply used the same melodic idea in two different ways; loud, fast, complex (la vie terrestre) followed by quiet, slow, simple (l'éternité bienheureuse). In that work the fast section is decidedly weak, but in *Les Offrandes* Messiaen succeeds by using brilliant orchestral colours with only minimal reference to a melodic phrase that occurs in the slow opening passage. Still, there is no doubt that the gentle outer sections speak with a far more individual voice, although they are distinct from each other in their effect because of the difference in their harmonic construction. 'The Cross', in spite of interruptions from mode III and its ending in mode II, begins from a tonal premiss—the melodic meandering against a held chord recalls Bartók—and the contrast between tonal and modal harmonies is what makes this passage so poignant. 'The Eucharist', by contrast, moves almost entirely between different transpositions of mode II chords, without ever superimposing one upon another (in Ex. 5b only the G♮ in bars 1 and 2 is foreign to the mode that surrounds it). In this way Messiaen conveys the unity and all-embracing nature of the Eucharist,

Ex.5(a)

Ex.5(b)

ending in the comfortable assurance of an added 6th. This chord more than any other has brought the critics down upon the composer crying 'saccharine sweetness' and 'sentimentality'. Judgment must remain the prerogative of the listener, who should prepare himself to meet the chord in any work of Messiaen at any time. If anyone requires intellectual reassurance, let him know that the chord of E major with added 6th, with which this work ends, is formed within mode II in its 2nd transposition—that is a semitone above the version printed above in Ex. 2. As Ex. 5a shows, Messiaen was already thinking in asymmetrical phrases. The changing bar-lengths of the first 2 sections of *Les Offrandes* are a symbol of the pain of the Cross and of the rejection of Christ in Sin, whereas in 'The Eucharist' the unchanging 4 beats in every bar reinforce the unity of the modal harmony.

In the same year (1931) that *Les Offrandes* was first performed Messiaen was appointed organist of the church of the Holy Trinity in Paris, a post that he still holds 44 years later. Marcel Dupré had recognized his genius for improvisation and had turned him in the direction of the king of instruments, on which Dupré himself was such a masterly improviser. In those 44 years Messiaen has produced no less than six large cycles of pieces for organ, amounting in all to some five hours of music. Three of the four pieces in his first cycle *L'Ascension* (1933) began life as part of an orchestral work and the process of transcription, the composer assures us, was a considerable labour. Although he now prefers to hear it in the orchestral version it is more convenient for us to investigate it in organ score and in any case the one movement he had to compose afresh (no. 3) illumines his attitude to the organ tradition of early 20th-century France.

In the first movement, 'Majesté du Christ demandant sa gloire à son Père', Messiaen exploits the tension between chords built from the chromatic modes and the conventional major and minor triads (Ex. 6).

Ex.6

R. Fonds et Anches 8', 4'   Péd. Fonds 16', 8', Tir.R.
P. Fonds 8'
G. Fonds 8'

Très lent et majestueux

+ 16′, 8′

The mode II chords of bar 1 resolve on to a major triad whose tonic note, E♮, is foreign to the mode. How much this contributes to the chord's cadential force is debatable; the B major chord heard at the end of bar 3, after two bars of mode III harmonies, is not foreign to that mode and yet its cadential force is strong. The alternation of tonic and dominant chords at the ends of the phrases indicates some respect at least for the value of conventional tonality although the asymmetry between phrases reduces its impact, as do the continuous syncopations. Gradually in the course of the piece the melody of bars 2–3 gains conviction until it finally explodes in a succession of six chords, ending triumphantly in E major. The second movement, 'Alléluias sereins', is the earliest example in Messiaen's music of the monody for which he has always felt a great affection. The inspiration here is plainsong, Messiaenized but easily recognizable (Ex. 7). Once more, in spite of the

Ex. 7

Pas trop modéré, et clair
G.P.R. Flûtes 8′, 4′, Octavin (2′)

modal outline, one note (F♮) is felt as a centre of attraction and indeed F major proves to be the key of the whole piece; once more, syncopations and asymmetric repetitions keep the listener guessing as to when the melody is going to end. Messiaen alternates this with a passage built on a much shorter pattern and goes on to present these two ideas again, in different textures. Finally the plainsong melody rings out on the pedal with 4′ and 1′ stops drawn. Historically speaking, the 'alternation' technique is justly applied to a melody inspired by plainsong but, given the textures with which Messiaen surrounds it, the piece comes over as both timeless and also definable within narrow temporal limits, the right hand figuration at the end harking back to a traditional model, the 'In Paradisum' of Fauré's *Requiem*.

As we mentioned above Messiaen wrote the third piece of the set, 'Transports de joie', specifically for the organ. It is widely felt to be inferior to the orchestral movement it replaced and certainly the latter is much more tightly constructed; but it is precisely the interplay of thematic and improvisatory elements that gives the organ piece its excitement. Furthermore it is a highly satisfying piece to play (Ex. 8).

Ex. 8

The layout of hands alone, feet alone, and finally both together may not be sophisticated, certainly not by comparison with some of Messiaen's later procedures, but it gives the player a profound satisfaction. Interesting from the technical point of view is the manner in which both the pedal phrase and the flurry of triplets are extended at their second appearance. In all the music of this early period Messiaen has a tendency to repeat his opening paragraph, a habit that can seem overemphatic if the material falls below the highest level of interest. Here the initial phrases are arresting enough and so abrupt that we welcome their extension, even if these too terminate in silence. Eventually figuration and pedal theme come together in an ecstatic passage, perfectly described by the piece's title (Ex. 9). In all it is a fruitful partner-

Ex. 9

ship between heart, head, and fingers, showing what Messiaen owed to Dupré and the French tradition behind him and what original uses he could make of that tradition.

The last of the four pieces, 'Prière du Christ montant vers son Père', owes nothing to anyone except Messiaen. Like the first piece it explores the relationship between the chromatic modes and conventional tonality, but the mood is entirely different. It is extremely slow—although in his own recording the composer goes rather beyond the text in stretching the final chord to some 57 seconds—and is largely built on the seventh and last of the chromatic modes. Messiaen has never used modes IV–VII as much as II and III, possibly because the 'charm of impossibilities' does not operate to the same extent in modes which allow more transpositions (Ex. 10). Mode VII, of 10 notes, comes nearest of them

Ex. 10

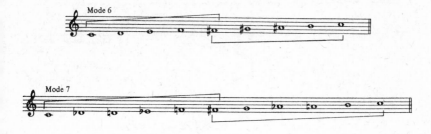

all to the chromatic scale and tends to provide the densest harmonic texture. In this piece we can almost feel the effort with which Christ drags himself out of the mire of this world to join his Father in heaven. Some may find such word-painting, or rather sense-painting, naïve but it is all of a piece with Messiaen's feeling for music not only as a concrete object to be manipulated but as a human activity to which, as in Ex. 8 above, the participants must be physically committed.

Finally we may note that, if the movement and atmosphere are akin to those of *Le Banquet céleste*, there is a distinct advance in the organization. Two ideas are juxtaposed, with variations but without any contrast other than that of direction. The opening (Ex. 11a) rises, the answer falls. The opening idea gains ground slowly so that by the end of its second appearance, in the middle of the movement, the cadential triad has risen from C major to E major. Together with this rise in pitch goes a shortening of the phrases: A—12 bars, B—12, A'–10, B'—8. Without prompt measures the movement is going to die of starvation, and the measures Messiaen takes are not only effective but are also the basis for one type of organisation on which he has relied throughout his career. As in the previous movement, a limb of the phrase is extended (Ex. 11) and this process also brings the music back to the original

Ex. 11(a)

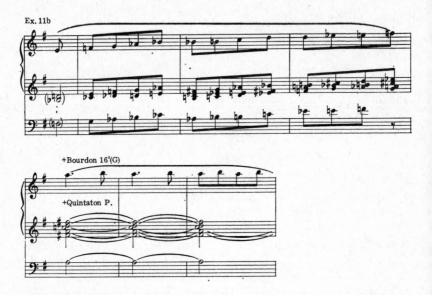

Ex. 11b

+Bourdon 16'(G)

+Quintaton P.

notes an octave higher. Impelled by a new energy, the piece rises to its inevitably celestial conclusion.

This answer is, essentially, a rhythmic one. So far in this study we have concentrated rather on harmony and melody because these are the facets of Messiaen's style that are likely first to engage the listener's attention, but it should be clear that in order to develop his musical style to deal with larger forms he needed to go beyond the very simple formal patterns, chiefly that of varied repetition, which we have seen so far. This development duly took place and in it rhythm played a crucial rôle.

First, we must be clear what Messiaen means by rhythm. According to him, rhythmic music is 'music which eschews repetition, bar lines, and equal divisions, which ultimately takes its inspiration from the movements of nature, movements which are free and unequal in length'. In other words, it is the very opposite of what an ordinary music-lover understands by the word. The unequal bar lengths in the first section of *Offrandes oubliées* (Ex. 5a) are one of the earliest signs of this preoccupation with what is free and unfettered by any prevailing 'tactus'. From the bar length this freedom soon spreads to the individual phrases and notes. It is achieved by either adding or subtracting values of an ordinary four-square rhythm; this dislocation sets up melodic tensions which the composer can then exploit.

The first work in which Messiaen explored these ideas at all systematically was the organ cycle *La Nativité du Seigneur* (1935), a work that has become almost a repertoire piece although the composer nowadays feels it is a little overrated by comparison with some of his other organ music. It must be said that these rhythmic ventures have probably played but a small part in the work's success, which has depended more on the composer's imaginative use of colour and on the rich harvest of melodies. To Messiaen, and so necessarily to us, the rhythms are vital. The techniques of addition or, rarely, subtraction can be applied either to a single note or, by the interpolation of notes, to a whole phrase. Two examples from *La Nativité* make this clear (Ex. 12).

Ex. 12(a)

Ex. 12b

On the penultimate C$\sharp$ of Ex. 12a the expected semiquaver is lengthened
to a dotted quaver, thereby increasing the power of the final G; it is, in
spirit, the kind of agogic accent that any sympathetic interpreter would
insert at this point although a composer's mandate is generally desirable
before one goes as far as Messiaen does here in trebling the length of a
note. In Ex. 12b the semiquavers marked with a cross have been
interpolated into a melody that already alternates between duple and
triple time. The whole section suggests with marvellous delicacy the
return of the shepherds from the manger, glorifying and praising God,
and the freedom of the rhythm marries with the momentary liberation
these men have found from their humdrum lives. The interpolations
seem to be made by the light of inspiration alone and very effective they
are, but given Messiaen's compulsive need to formalize his inspiration
we need not be surprised to find them eventually harnessed to a system.

Some of this rhythmic freedom undoubtedly stems from that of the
French language. Already in 1930 Messiaen had written his *Trois
mélodies*, one of the works with which he won his *premier prix* from the
Conservatoire, and as the central song had set, for the only time in his
life, one of his mother's poems. The word setting in this song follows
the precepts of Debussy as displayed in *Pelléas*, with repeated notes
and one juxtaposition of triplet and duplet, the whole imitating the rise
and fall of ordinary conversation. In the other two songs of the set, to
poems by the composer, the word setting is solid by comparison and he
does not achieve a consistently fluent style until his *Poèmes pour Mi*
(1936) written for his first wife, Claire Delbos. This fluency is apparent
from the outset (Ex. 13). Rightly sung, the recitative generates tremen-

dous tension and the music seems indeed to be 'transformed' by light as the line explodes like a firework and falls gracefully to earth. But the melodic line and the singing of it are by no means the whole secret. As so often with Messiaen, freedom and discipline are made to interact. In Ex. 13a the right hand of the piano plays, in mode III, a series of six chords, the first five of which are then repeated; in the left hand mode II harmonies are disposed in a series of five chords, repeated intact. For the first bar the two parts move in rhythmic canon a crotchet apart. In bar 2 the first three chords of the right hand manoeuvre into a position from which they can precipitate the entry of the voice, and they do this by abandoning rhythmic subtleties and modulating from a combination of modes II and III into a wholehearted mode VI. In the build-up to the second recitative the number of the precipitating chords is increased from three to six, and in that to the third (Ex. 13b) the embryonic organization of the rhythm is fully developed: the group of six chords in the right hand is repeated five times while that of five chords in the left hand is repeated six times, and throughout this cycle the two hands maintain their rhythmic canon. Understandably, after this *tour de force* the number of the precipitating chords is further increased to nine.

We may at this point pause to ask whether this sort of discipline is likely to convey itself to the listener, whether indeed he needs to know about it in order to appreciate the music. An example from *La Nativité* may help us (Ex. 14). Here a phrase ten semiquavers long in the right

Ex. 14

hand is set over one nine semiquavers long in the left, and at the tenth bar
(where the example ends) the original pattern would recur. The effect is
simple; the technique registers at once with the listener but one may
doubt whether he feels any real excitement, as the markings 'crescendo
molto' and 'rallentando molto' suggest he should. In fact it is too simple,
because every note and every chord is kept to its original length and the
music soon becomes predictable. What saves the passages in Ex. 13 is
that the rhythmic canon, although binding the two strands together in
time, cuts across their melodic outlines. Whether the listener knows this
or not is surely unimportant. But it is nevertheless true that without
this discipline the apparent freedom of Ex. 13b could well degenerate
into chaos. On a quite different level is the purely personal satisfaction
that Messiaen derives from writing both *La Nativité* and *Poèmes pour Mi*
as cycles of nine pieces because 9 is the number symbolic of maternity.

These two works, together with the next song-cycle, *Chants de terre
et de ciel* (1938), represent a plateau in the composer's harmonic and
melodic style. The chromatic modes are omnipresent and this stylistic
unity helps to make all three works easily attractive to the listener,
although *Chants de terre et de ciel* in particular presents formidable
problems to the singer. Even if the modes began for Messiaen as
entities of harmonic colour, they often give rise to germane melodic
formulae which recur from work to work. One of these is derived, so
Messiaen assures us, from the seemingly unlikely source of *Boris
Godunov*, but remade to accord with mode II. Another is simply a
series of descending chords in whatever the current mode may be. This
may sound uncomfortably simplistic but once again the critic of the
theory can be confounded with example. *La Nativité* is crowned by the
largest piece of the cycle, 'Dieu parmi nous', which begins with an
exultant invocation in mode IV (Ex. 15a), guaranteed to bring any

Très modéré

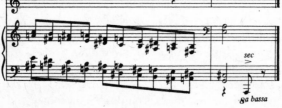

(la joie) est   re - ve - nu - e.

congregation out of religious reverie. The pedal theme, in mode II, gains in contrast by using all four of the notes excluded from this first transposition of the mode (E♭, E♮, A♮, B♭). Ex. 15b proclaims the same mood in the same mode—a major 3rd higher than printed in Ex. 10—but this is an ending, of the last of the *Poèmes pour Mi*. No doubt it is perfectly possible to write rubbish using these chromatic modes, as it is under any other system, and Messiaen's success in manipulating them must be judged not from the standpoint of theoretical purity but quite simply from the result. The C♯ and G♮ in the final minim chord of 15b are foreign to mode IV; do these alien notes help in halting the downward rush of the music, are they exciting, are they right? Let the reader play them and judge for himself.

1936 was a rather special year for Messiaen. At the age of 28 he was appointed a professor at the École Normale and at the Schola Cantorum, and was one of four young composers who together formed a group under the title 'La jeune France'. According to their manifesto the group 'propose the dissemination of works that are youthful, free, as far removed from revolutionary formulae as from academic formulae ... their only unqualified agreement is in the common desire to be satisfied with nothing less than sincerity, breadth of feeling, and artistic good faith'. These words suggest a distaste not only for the principles of the Second Viennese school but also for the effusions of Satie and Les Six, many of which no doubt seemed to come straight from the sleeve. Of Messiaen's heart there has never been any doubt, and from its wholeness and oneness springs the basic unity of his style. But in that unity there are many mansions, each one furnished differently according to the varying interactions of his heart with his no less active head.

His third organ cycle, *Les Corps glorieux* (1939), is a perfect microcosm of this interaction. Between the seven pieces and inside them there are the extreme contrasts that Messiaen loves. Monody, already present in the second movement of *L'Ascension* but almost entirely absent from *La Nativité*, returns in the first, third, and fifth pieces; there are mixed chromatic modes in the second and third, a revelling in organ colours in the sixth, while the central piece, 'Combat de la Mort et de la Vie', expands the block contrast of the early *Diptyque* into something monumental. Messiaen also refers back to *L'Ascension* in giving the cycle a quiet ending, but hidden in this apparently grey portrait of the Mystery of the Holy Trinity are new techniques and new perspectives which were soon to lift him off the plateau into more rarefied regions (Ex. 16). In honour of the Trinity the piece is both

Ex. 16

R. bourdon 16' et octavin (2')
P. flûte 8'
Péd. bourdon 32' tir. R.

vertically and horizontally tripartite—Ex. 16 shows the first third of it. Furthermore, each third is divided into three, as can be seen by looking at the melody in the middle part, so that the overall plan is that of a nine-fold Kyrie. The melody is centred firmly on D but the right hand arabesques are, on the composer's admission, almost atonal. Most interesting of all is the pedal line, where Messiaen employs a version of 'râgavardhana', one of the Hindu rhythms that are to be a constant feature of his music from now on; the initial series of six values (4,4,4,2,3,2) forms one of his most frequent rhythmic patterns, followed here by two other rhythms of similar origin. This pedal line is repeated five times but each repetition includes small differences and the length of the pauses between them is not regulated by anything except the free will of the composer. He arranges them so that the D♮s in the bass coincide, either actually or by implication, no less than ten times with those of the melody. One could, just, call this composition by formula. Certainly one could accuse it of being at one and the same time revolutionary and academic. If, nevertheless, it works, then we must look for the reason in the composer's sincerity, in his breadth of feeling, and in his artistic good faith.

MESSIAEN finished *Les Corps glorieux* on 25 August 1939. Nine days later France was at war. He joined the French army and in June 1940 was captured by the Germans at Nancy while trying to escape on an old bicycle with no tyres. He was transferred to Stalag VIII A in Silesia carrying, among little else, the Brandenburg concertos, scores by Beethoven, Ravel, and Stravinsky, and Berg's *Lyric Suite*. The outcome of this isolation was a masterpiece. *Quatuor pour la fin du temps*, finished in January 1941, was given its first performance in the same month by the composer with three fellow prisoners playing clarinet, violin, and cello.

It is tempting to interpret the title as meaning 'Quartet for the end of metre'; bar-lines are often no more than aids to ensemble and a means of reducing accidentals. In fact the title comes from a passage in the Apocalypse and the work is dedicated to the Angel 'who lifts his hand towards the heaven saying "There shall be no more time"'. And it must frequently have seemed, in the endless boredom of that camp, that the Angel's prophecy had been fulfilled. Certainly the two accompanied solos for the stringed instruments and the third movement for clarinet alone cannot be appreciated by, could not have been written by a man in a hurry.

From the technical viewpoint the Quartet contains two innovations which can hardly be overemphasized. Firstly, the introduction of bird-song. At the opening of the first movement, 'Liturgie de cristal', a black-bird and a nightingale celebrate the arrival of dawn (Ex. 17). At the same

Ex. 17

time the cello plays a 5-note ostinato stretched over a rhythmic pedal of 15 values; and the piano plays a 29-note ostinato stretched over a rhythmic pedal of 17 values—Messiaen's reworking of the Hindu rhythm 'râgavardhana' (see pedal part of Ex. 16). The structure of this movement therefore depends, once more, on a combination of freedom and discipline, simplicity and complexity, and it is noticeable that the end of the movement is determined not, as one might expect, by the fulfilment of this complexity but by the free and simple birds, who just 'sign off'.

The second of these innovations is less revolutionary. We have seen, in *Offrandes oubliées*, Messiaen's delight in unequal phrases, carried further in the works that followed. This desire of the heart is now brought under control by the head and allied to the 'charm of impossibilities' (Ex. 18). The rhythm of each bar is what Messiaen calls a 'non-retrograde' rhythm; whether you read it from left to right or from right

Ex. 18

(lointain)

pp (legato) + 8ᵛᵃ bassa

to left it remains the same. With the aid of such palindromic rhythms he pursues his quest, 'éloigner le temporel'. Theory aside, there is nothing in this work 'difficult' for the listener if he is patient and has no immovable objection to being surprised. Five thousand prisoners heard and, we are told, greatly appreciated the first performance, given on a piano whose keys kept sticking and in a temperature of −30°C.

In Messiaen's next work, however, the level of dissonance rises somewhat sharply. *Visions de l'Amen* (1943) for two pianos was his first major work after being repatriated and appointed Professor of Harmony at the Paris Conservatoire. It is not hard to see in this set of seven pieces a celebration of personal freedom, but this is to take a rather superficial view. Nearer the truth is that among his first pupils on his return to Paris was the pianist Yvonne Loriod, now his second wife, whose 'transcendent virtuosity' allowed him to write with assurance music that was both technically and aesthetically difficult. Furthermore, the two-piano medium led him to conceive a work that is more dramatic than anything he had written so far.

One obvious aspect of this dramatic approach is his use of a single main theme, the 'theme of the Creation'. It is basic to the outer movements but makes only intermittent appearances in some of the others, as a coda to no. 3, as a rhythm in no. 4 and as one element in the episodic construction of no. 5; it is absent from nos. 2 and 6. Its effect on the themes and figurations round it is minimal so that it stands like a land-

Ex. 19(a)

Très lent, mystérieux et solennel (♪ = 50)

Piano 1 *pppp*

(garder la pédale forte jusqu'à la fin)
Piano 2 *ppp*

8ᵛᵃ bassa

mark, a reference point among the exotic proliferation of ideas. In the
first movement, 'Amen de la création', the theme slowly reveals itself
in one mighty crescendo lasting some 6½ minutes, decorated throughout
by an organized chaos of bells. The last movement, 'Amen de la
consommation', takes over from where the first left off, but now the
speed is more than doubled and the bells sound below as well as above.

Ex. 19(b)

* Attaquer staccato et mettre en même temps la pédale forte. Chaque note bien marquée. Sonorité de cloches; laisser résonner.

** Attaquer martelé, en liant avec la pédale.

Although, on paper, this movement is more than three times the length of the first, in performance it should last only about 1½ minutes more. Messiaen is almost content to rely on this temporal manipulation and any variations occur within the basically jubilant atmosphere (Ex. 19a, b, c).

Ex. 19d is taken from the fifth movement, at the point where the rhythmic organization in the first piano part reaches an apogee of complexity. Two palindromic rhythms (marked inside square brackets) are presented successively, each one in triple canon with itself at a semiquaver's distance, and a further aspect of this symmetry can be seen in the shape of the rhythms themselves (35853 and 43734 expressed in units of a demisemiquaver), in which the central value is the sum of its two predecessors/successors. The first piano part in both 19a and 19b is similarly regulated, though in both cases the canons are double not triple and the rhythm of 19b is not palindromic, being the version of 'râgavardhana' already quoted in Ex. 16. Through all this runs the dramatic opposition of the two pianos. 'I have entrusted to the first piano,' says Messiaen, 'the rhythmic difficulties, the chord-clusters, everything that involves speed, charm, and sonority. I have entrusted to the second piano the main melody, the thematic elements, everything that demands emotion and power.'

33

The piano was to be protagonist or participant in nearly every work of Messiaen's for the next 15 years. Ten months after the first performance of *Visions de l'Amen* he began a cycle of pieces for piano solo which sums up his achievement until this point in its synthesis of strict rhythmic organization, wide ranges of colour, extremes of speed and slowness, all in the service of a personal but hardly narrow view of the second person of the Trinity and the relations between Him and both the material and immaterial world. But *Vingt Regards sur l'enfant-Jésus* (1944) is not merely a compendium of techniques and 'recherché' sonorities. If it is a masterpiece it is because Messiaen possesses the

Ex. 19(d)

* Percuté, sonorité de gong; flageller les touches (comme un pizzicato)
   en mettant en même temps la pédale forte.

genius to give coherence to a work lasting 2 hours, that taxes to the
utmost the stamina of the performer and his audience.

Partly this coherence is achieved by good, old-fashioned tonality. Of
the twenty pieces, four in the first half are centred round F♯ major
(nos. 1, 4, 5, 6) and three in the second (15, 19, 20). It is even possible
to detect a kind of ABA' structure in the way this tonality is positioned
within the cycle. Messiaen also goes beyond the single main theme of

Visions de l'Amen and brings in five themes at different points in the work. One, the 'Theme of chords', is hardly a theme, just a succession of four 4-part chords involving all twelve notes of the scale, but the rest have recognizable melodic shapes and of these by far the most important is the 'Theme of God'. It appears in seven of the twenty contemplations and in its varied forms presents a musical parallel to the figure of God, who embraces all things and yet remains always the same (Ex. 20). Ex. 20c is the sort of passage that has caused pain to those devotees of the modern music for whom the perfect cadence is an obscenity. Messiaen's achievement is not so much in daring to write such music, although

Ex. 20(a)

Regard du Père

Extrêmement lent. mystérieux, avec amour (♪ des triolets = 60)

(Thème de Dieu) 8va bassa

Ex. 20(b)

Modéré (♪ = 138)

(Thème de Dieu)

'daring' is the word, as in making it a logical part of a work that also includes such a passage as the opening of the second contemplation (Ex. 21). We can see that what, in *Visions de l'Amen*, had been decora-

Ex. 21   Regard de l'étoile

tion now stands as substance. The first two bars and the last bar each build up to chords containing all twelve notes but such is the logic of the progression, from a rising phrase, through a falling one, to some sort of equilibrium in the repeated C♮s, that we appreciate the chords as no more than colouring in an independently organized design. The high 9ths and 7ths of bar 2 are sounds new to piano music at this time though their origin may be traced back to the piano chords in Ex. 17. Less original perhaps are the imitations of oboes, trombones, and tam-tams in nos. 14 and 16 where Messiaen follows the lead of Debussy in treating the piano as an orchestra; indeed he claims 'it is possible to make sounds on a piano that are more orchestral than those of an orchestra'.

Among other contributors to the work's unity are the chromatic modes and birdsong which, in the eighth piece, is allotted for the first time an unaccompanied or rather non-accompanying rôle. The rhythmic subtleties too reinforce the impression of confident eccentricity, of a vast universe minutely explored. In particular the added values and persistent asymmetry of phrases keep the listener listening forward to some kind of resolution. The asymmetries are not those of, say, Bartók's *Dances in Bulgarian rhythm* where a metre of 2+2+2+3 is employed regularly. With Messiaen one is never absolutely sure where the added values are going to come. This insecurity is especially valuable in some of the slower pieces (4, 15, 19) where the harmony is very sweet and simple and banality is perpetually imminent; the duality between the harmony and the rhythm not only tinges the sweetness with an acceptable acidity but makes us hear both constituents that much more clearly.

The old conflict between head and heart, complexity and simplicity, discipline and freedom is joined memorably in the ninth piece, 'Regard du temps', where heart and head take turns (Ex. 22). The two contrasted textures may be understood as deriving from the paradox which Messiaen places at the head of the piece—'time sees the birth inside itself of Him who is eternal'—but they are also in a direct line of

Ex. 22

Regard du temps

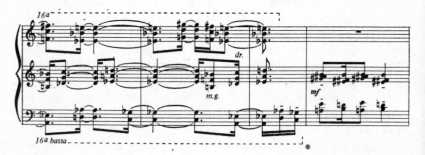

development from the friction of opposites set up in *Diptyque* and *Offrandes oubliées*. The opening theme, 'short, cold, strange', is not subject to any mathematical system. The first two of its three phrases are quoted above in bars 1, 2 and 7, 8, and its third and final one comes immediately after the end of Ex. 22. At its next appearance phrases one and two are juxtaposed and the time after that the three phrases are played continuously. Alternating with this melodic element throughout is the rhythmic canon which begins at the end of bar 2, the three parts entering at a quaver's distance. The first three values of the canon, of 8, 4, 8 semiquavers, undergo proportional changes, first to 6, 3, 6, then to 10, 5, 10 semiquavers. After the continuous presentation of the first two phrases of the theme the rhythmic canon goes one better by juxtaposing all three proportional versions in their original order. After this the theme returns complete and the piece ends with the initial 8, 4, 8 scheme of the canon followed by just the last four chords of the theme, and crowned by a little flourish producing a 12-note chord.

Messiaen himself describes 'Regard du temps' as a mysterious piece. The texture of the canon looks bizarre on paper but in fact is spell-binding (for its origin as accompanying material see Ex. 19b). But one of the most exciting properties of *Vingt Regards* is that tunefulness keeps breaking in. To anyone puzzled or repelled by the mysteries of 'Regard du temps' let this passage, the final bars of the whole work, speak of 'the triumph of love and joy':

Ex. 23

Between these two monuments of piano writing Messiaen had been engaged on a commission to write a choral work and it says something for his intellectual vigour at this period that only 8 days after completing it he began work on *Vingt Regards*. The *Trois petites Liturgies* for 18 female voices and orchestra was his first original orchestral work since *L'Ascension* 11 years earlier. Given a choice of two epithets that would describe it, one might choose 'melodic' and 'colourful'; a work that was surely bound to find a welcome in the grey days of 1945.

The first performance, given in Paris on 21 April, less than a month after that of *Vingt Regards*, produced a riot. It was followed by a sustained barrage of criticism in the press, dubbed the 'bataille des liturgies'. In Claude Rostand's description: 'in short, the whole musical world in Paris suddenly went mad, a madness for which, possibly, the end of the Occupation was partly responsible and which had not been seen since the great days of Stravinsky. It was a kind of dance of glory and death around Messiaen, the hero crucified. . .' If the critics were outraged, the audience was enthusiastic. So one asks 'why were the critics outraged?' On the musical level the melody and colour combine in such surprising ways. The melodic outlines are often tonal or pentatonic but the colour regularly seems to work against the melodic assumptions, so that one hears the major triads with new ears—colour here does the job of rhythm in the slower pieces of *Vingt Regards*. The sounds of piano, vibraphone, celeste, maracas, Chinese cymbal, and especially the ethereal whistling of the 'ondes Martenot', conspire to seduce the objective analyst, inviting him to bask in the luxuriance of an A major triad. The French critics, feeling their intelligences threatened, struck back. On the textual level too many were offended by the blend of psalms and botany, of astronomy and the *Song of Songs*. The composer remained undisturbed, if surprised, by the whole affair and his confidence has been borne out by the work's subsequent popularity. It is a delightful and undemanding work for the listener, retaining the tonally based sensuousness of Messiaen's earlier music but looking forward in its plainsong patterns, Hindu rhythms, and embellishments of birdsong.

The four works of the years 1944–8 (*Trois petites Liturgies, Vingt Regards, Harawi,* and *Turangalîla*) together form a second stylistic plateau. They mark a period of assimilation, or even an 'impasse'. One need not subscribe to the theory that for a composer development is all to see that the diversity of techniques Messiaen had now embraced could endanger the unity of his style. In particular the contrast between tonality or modality and total atonality had to be handled with care; there was always the risk of the more conventional sections sounding naïve. In *Vingt Regards* and *Trois petites Liturgies* the inspiration is generally so overwhelming, and in the latter the sheer sound so marvellous, that there seems to be no problem after all. But in *Harawi, chant d'amour et de mort* (1945) the most ardent enthusiast may have his doubts. It is the third and so far the last of Messiaen's song cycles, all written for the dramatic soprano Marcelle Bunlet, and also the first piece in the trilogy of works inspired by the legend of Tristan. Any attempt to reconcile the love/death paradox may be expected to produce an enigmatic work. Yet this is not the main reason for *Harawi*'s enigmatic quality, which lies more in the discrepancies between modal and atonal passages. The complex, dissonant sections are so arresting and original that it is sometimes hard to accept the points of modal repose with equanimity. Comparison of the following example from 'Adieu' (Ex. 24) with Ex. 22 will demonstrate the relative width of

linguistic experience that, in *Harawi*, is often compressed into one statement. The languages of *Vingt Regards* are just as distinct but Messiaen had not felt it necessary there to give them such a stringent test of compatibility. The whole song consists of six alternations of the material of Ex. 24 with extensions and variations, but the catalyst is missing that would make the two styles into one experience; one senses the disturbing mystery of 'Regard du temps' without its beauty or excitement.

The *Turangalîla Symphony* (1948), the second work in the Tristan trilogy, also shows on occasion the strains of elaborate synthesis, but the problems were easier for the composer to solve, chiefly because of the vast orchestra that he chose to employ. This made it possible to play tonal and non-tonal ideas simultaneously, rather as in *Visions de l'Amen*, with the added advantage that differences in timbre keep the ideas clear and distinct. At the same time, the ear is continually being drawn away from the simple to attend to the complex. From the ten movements of the symphony a wealth of illustrations suggest themselves. The beginning of the sixth movement, 'Jardin du sommeil d'amour', is a particularly beautiful example (Ex. 25). The whole movement is an extension of the principle already seen in *Le Banquet céleste*, of evoking an atmosphere to which the following variations are wholly subservient. The texture could not be more straightforward. Strings and ondes martenot play the theme; piano, flute, clarinet, and percussion decorate

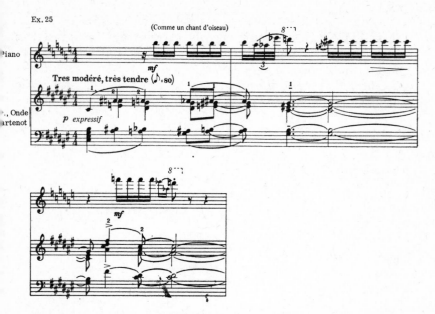

Ex. 25

it. The theme moves to and fro between two inversions of mode II (the chords marked 1 belong to that on C♯, those marked 2 to that on C♮), but overall each phrase can clearly be heard as a delayed dominant cadence. Over this, the decorations are seemingly arbitrary in pitch, although throughout the movement they keep to their characteristic outlines. Given this strong textural identity, or duality, Messiaen feels able to introduce into the decorative patterns some typically complex rhythmic formulae which again draw the ear away from the underlying theme. Not that the theme is at all square or obvious. Even if, as in *Le Banquet céleste*, the first phrase is at once repeated, the climactic note is raised the second time, and in any case the phrase is an asymmetrical 35 quavers long.

Only very rarely, as at fig. 13 in the fifth movement, do we become uncomfortably aware of the 19th century leering over Messiaen's shoulder; for the most part he bends tonality to his will with splendid effect. As in *Vingt Regards*, F♯ major may be regarded as the overall tonic, prepared by the firm D♭ major of the fifth movement. The F♯ major of the sixth is also firm but so slow and dreamlike that, even with experience of 'Combat de la mort et de la vie', we are not tempted to mistake it for the end; while in the eighth movement F♯ major is destroyed at the final moment. So the last movement is heard to be the last even as it begins: its triadic theme in F♯ major recalls the fifth movement as do the driving triplets and brash orchestration, and the theme of the sixth movement, the only other one in F♯ major, receives a glorious apotheosis on full orchestra. The final chord of F♯ has been well earned and clearly foreseen.

The symphony is constructed round two well-contrasted cyclic themes, the first (Ex. 26a) static, fitted for rounding off long arguments

Ex. 26(a)

Ex. 26(b)

—as at the end of the fifth movement—the second (Ex. 26b), for all its gentle charm, dynamic in the way that it unfolds into the minor 3rd. We may feel, as some critics have, that Ex. 26a is unnecessarily emphatic, and certainly the end of the fifth movement sounds dangerously final. Ex. 26b, without drawing attention to itself, plays its part in fashioning the melodic material of the symphony and in its final achievement of concord may be taken as a symbol of the tonal struggle in the work as a whole.

The title of the symphony brings together two Hindu words; *Lîla* 'game, in the sense of divine action on the cosmos' and *Turanga* 'the passage of time', which Messiaen associates with rhythm. It is fitting then to end discussion of *Turangalîla* by taking a look at his rhythmic preoccupations and how he uses orchestral colour to make these preoccupations not only plain but palatable. The second section of the Introduction, detonated by a piano cadenza, is built on the continuous re-ordering of five coloured rhythms (Ex. 27). (a), a Hindu rhythm, marks a pattern of 2, 3, 4, 4 semiquavers followed by 4 semiquavers' rest, (b) is the succession of Hindu rhythms already shown in Ex. 16, while (c) counts out the basic semiquaver units in recurrent groups of 10. (d) is a series of palindromic rhythms; their extent is marked in square brackets, the central pivot with a cross. Finally (e) decreases by single semiquaver units from 17 to 7, returns to 17, then continues to oscillate between the two extremes. Of course, the audience is not meant to appreciate the mathematics in detail, but by the end of 69 bars it is impossible to be totally unaware of the fearful symmetries that underlie this superbly exciting passage; and both awareness and excitement are nourished by the rich orchestral colours in which the symmetries are presented. (See over for Ex. 27.)

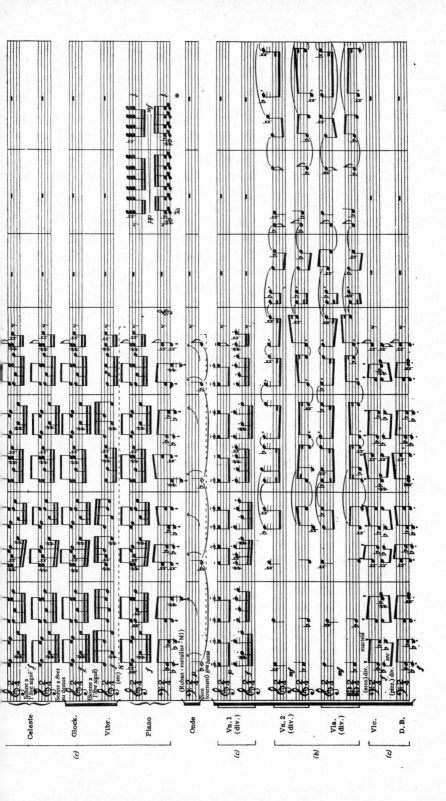

1948–1958

MESSIAEN finished *Turangalîla* in November 1948, a few days before his fortieth birthday. But by the time of its first and triumphant performance in Boston a year later he had moved right away from tonality both as a local and an overall constructive force, right away indeed from birdsong and Hindu rhythms. There are passing references to tonality in the third of the *Cinq Rechants* (1948) for unaccompanied chorus which complete the Tristan trilogy, and Hindu rhythms play a part in both this work and the piano piece *Cantéjodjayâ* of the following year, but with another piano piece, *Mode de valeurs et d'intensités*, written at Darmstadt in 1949, Messiaen conducted what he has since admitted to be an experiment, more interesting perhaps as a signpost to follow than as an experience to enjoy. One must say 'perhaps' because not everyone would agree. The composer, with pardonable pride, recalls a moment at Darmstadt the following year when he put on the newly released recording of this work. Two of his pupils 'put the record on again and again, some twenty times, their attention gripped and their eyes shining. "Here," they kept saying, "is the first complete and methodical exploration of the universe of sound such as we have always dreamt about".' One of those two was the 21-year-old Stockhausen.

In place of chromatic modes or any other of his well-tried devices Messiaen here turns to a strict determinism that embraces not only the actual notes of the scale but also their length, the type of attack with which they are played, and their loudness (although Schoenberg's 12-note system may have been the inspiration, it plays no part directly). Altogether the pianist must manipulate 36 notes, 24 note values, 12 types of attack, and 7 dynamic levels, the whole being laid out on three staves, each of which combines the above elements differently. Here are the three divisions and the first 7 bars of the piece (Ex. 28). All this looks

Ex. 28(a)

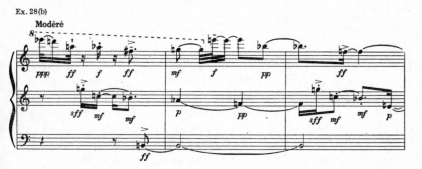

Ex. 28(b)

complicated and rather arid. But there are a number of accepted musical principles underlying Messiaen's permutations of notes. For example, every individual note has a different dynamic marking in each of the three divisions so that even on a monochrome instrument the levels are kept distinct; the dynamics also take account of the evanescent sound of the instrument, the lowest division being made louder on the whole than the upper ones because the notes are longer and also because Messiaen wants the low notes to colour the upper ones with their resonance; finally, the longer, lower notes are played less frequently than the shorter, higher ones so that there is a textual identity, a 'gestalt'. Even so, he does not allow this to become too obvious, arranging the divisions, and especially the two lower ones, to overlap in pitch. To end the piece he even makes a traditionally dramatic gesture: as it began with the high E♭, *ppp*, so it ends with the low C♯, *sfff*.

But, successful experiment or not, the point of interest is surely that Messiaen felt he had to make it. Ex. 25 is beautiful but it is hard to see where it can lead. Perhaps Messiaen himself gave a clue in the evasive answer he made around 1966 to a question from Claude Samuel:

Q: Among your instrumental compositions, do you think the *Turangalîla Symphony* is the best summary of your musical aims?

A: It is one of the richest in fine passages, it is also the most melodic, the warmest, the most dynamic and colourful.

But not the best summary of his musical aims! The astringency of *Mode de valeurs* and of the three other *Études de rythme* for piano may still appear extreme today, but they had an entirely beneficial effect on his subsequent work, dispelling some of the more enervating and soporific perfumes of *Turangalîla*.

After a year's almost total banishment, the birds return in *Messe de la Pentecôte* (1950) for organ. This is a compendium of the improvisations of Messiaen the practising organist and therefore contains a number of phrases recognizable from his earlier works, even if they are often transformed in rhythm and colour; their pitch, however, stays the same, indicating that his mind was prompted by his fingers. On the other hand, the organization is anything but improvisatory. Hindu rhythms and rhythms taken from classical Greek poetry dominate the first three of the five movements, together with the technique of 'interversions' which he had already tried out in one of the *Études de rythme*. He takes a limited set of durations and permutates their order, often in two or three parts simultaneously. Given the same set for each part, the beginnings of each permutation, whatever they may be, will always coincide; in this way the parts are guaranteed both unity with and independence from each other. With only two parts the pattern is sometimes hard to hear because there will tend to be coincidence at places other than the beginning of the sets, but with three parts it is clear enough (Ex. 29). The rhythmic set is simply of 1, 2, 3, 4, 5 semi-

Ex. 29

quavers. The strands are distinguished not only by rhythm but also by timbre and by harmony. The right hand is in mode III, the left in mode IV, while the pedal plays an ostinato. This type of harmonic organization goes back to *La Nativité* but here it has a new subtlety. The ostinato changes at its fourth appearance, omitting the low C♮ which 'happens' to be the only note common to all three parts. The omission is immediately rectified in the most direct manner, which could have been comic if it had not been so carefully prepared.

Elsewhere in this movement, as in Ex. 27c, two-part interversions are regulated by continuous semiquavers in the third part. A more imaginative solution to this problem, of supplying a pulse against which the complex rhythms can work, appears in the final 'Sortie', where Messiaen replaces continuous semiquavers by a chorus of larks (Ex. 30). The lower parts again are rigidly disciplined in both rhythm and harmony. The left hand plays a series of diminishing values in mode IV, the pedal a series of increasing values in a mode VI ostinato. Altogether this passage is a marvellously fluid application of the notion of 'personnages rythmiques' which Messiaen developed in analysing *Le Sacre du printemps*: he likens the behaviour of some of the themes in this work to that of three actors on a stage, where one acts, one is acted upon, and one merely listens—paralleled in the music by those ideas that grow, those that contract, and those, often ostinati, that are un-changing. The concept of a cadenza-like introduction to a full passage looks back to *Turangalîla* from which, in fact, the phrase in brackets is taken note for note.[1]

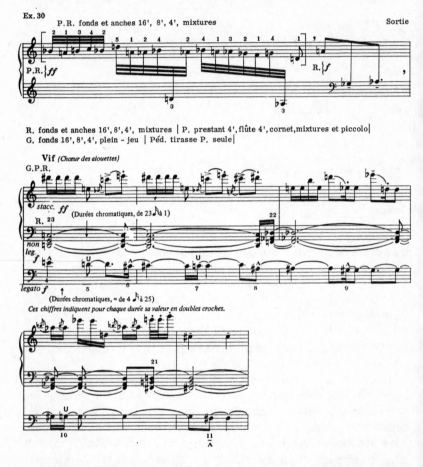

Ex. 30

Having rid himself of a backlog of improvisatory ideas Messiaen now wrote *Livre d'orgue* (1951) which looks back little further than the four *Études de rythme*, and develops some of the experiments contained therein. In particular, principles of interversion are now applied to Hindu rhythms, hitherto left untouched, and the sound-durations are exploited more sparingly and perhaps more effectively than in *Mode*

[1] See *Turangalîla II*, 3 bars before 32.

de valeurs. The layout of the seven pieces is a clear embodiment of the composer's heart/head dichotomy. The first two pieces live by rhythm and colour alone. Accordingly, the third piece, 'Les Mains de l'abîme', begins and ends with a terrifying directness and solidity. The fourth, 'Chants d'oiseaux', is a pastoral interlude, to allow for the recovery of audience and organist alike before the fifth, in which Messiaen once more taxes the plain man's understanding with a long trio of impenetrable rhythmic virtuosity. In the last two pieces the threads are drawn together: loudness, directness, and textural uniformity in the sixth piece, delicacy, colour, birdsong, and rhythmic complexity in the last.

While proud of his intellectual achievement in writing the fifth movement, the composer thinks 'Les Mains de l'abîme' the most successful of the seven and certainly it is a spine-chilling evocation of the text from Habakkuk: 'l'abîme a jeté son cri! la profondeur a levé ses deux mains' (Ex. 31). The consolation offered in the following pages is

Ex. 31

Tutti *fff* | G.P.R. fonds et anches 16', 8', 4', mixtures | Péd. fonds et anches 16', 8', 4', 32' | tous accouplements et tirasses|

(Interversions sur 3 rythmes hindous: manthikâ 1ᵉʳ, forme exagérée, ne change pas– manthikâ 2ᵉ et mallatâla augmentent chacun d'une ♪ par valeur, à chaque répétition.)

Bien modéré

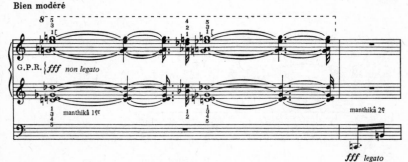

swept aside by a cadenza and the voice of the abyss continues its terrible cry to the end. In broadness of effect this piece looks forward to the 'monumental' Messiaen of *Et exspecto*, when he was again inspired by the visionary language of the Scriptures.

In the last piece of the set, 'Soixante-quatre Durées', we see another, quite different matching of a rigid formula with the highest inspiration. On the manuals note values (in demi-semiquavers) are arranged as follows: 61, 62, 63, 64 / 4, 3, 2, 1 / 57, 58, 59, 60 / 8, 7, 6, 5 etc., the piece ending with the series 33, 34, 35, 36 / 32, 31, 30, 29 (Ex. 32). Even if this

Ex. 32

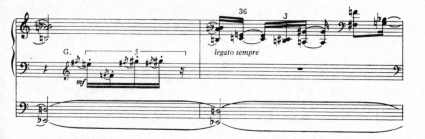

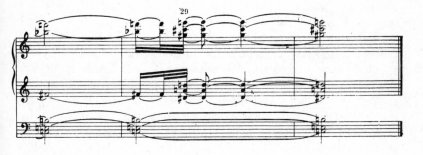

55

doesn't look like organ music it is nevertheless comfortable and highly satisfying to play. The end really sounds like the end, a more important consideration by far than the fact that the last two chords employ all twelve semitones without duplication.

Since his repatriation in 1942 Messiaen had composed with no appreciable pause for 9 years, producing some 8 hours of music including the vast score of *Turangalîla*. In the 5 years 1952–6 he wrote only two works, lasting together under 40 minutes. This sudden fall in production can possibly be explained in part by the tragic illness of his first wife who by the mid-1950s was no longer able to communicate with the outside world. While it would be tendentious, as well as impertinent, to insist on any such connection, Messiaen has admitted that he finds refuge in birdsong 'when my uselessness is brutally revealed to me and all the musical languages of the world seem to be merely an effort of patient research . . .' At all events his compositions until *Chronochromie* of 1960 are based in varying degrees on birdsong, a revolutionary concept which has not, unlike so many of his, been taken up by the avant-garde, indeed has been viewed in some quarters either as non-composition or as near proof of imbecility.

The first fruit of this absorption was *Réveil des oiseaux* (1953), which contains no material except the songs of 38 birds. The first problem in composing such a work is obviously that of form. All the traditional frames of tonality, modality, and rhythmic organization—Greek and Hindu rhythms and interversions—all these Messiaen abandoned, trusting in the beauty and variety of the material itself whose only noticeable formal characteristic is a tendency towards repeated notes and brief ostinati. The only frames otherwise are the piano/orchestra contrast and one supplied by nature herself. The work 'lasts' from midnight to midday, in which period there are two climaxes: the grand dawn chorus at 4 a.m. and a long piano cadenza just before midday which incorporates the songs of 15 different birds. Within this general plan Messiaen's success or failure is decided by the timing, placing, and scoring of his material.

This brings us to a second problem, that of authenticity. Messiaen claims that in *Réveil des oiseaux* the birdsongs are reproduced exactly, although he recognizes that this exactness has been much questioned and that in any case it is unattainable. Birds sing higher and faster than any humanly operated instruments can play and the melodic intervals they produce are often infinitesimal. By 'exactly' he means that he has reproduced the original material in terms that humans can perform and understand; that is, the internal relationships of the birdsongs have been as far as possible maintained, even though the whole is now lower, slower, and based on a smallest melodic interval of a semitone.

Réveil des oiseaux compares with *Mode de valeurs* in its dedication to a single principle. That said, we can hardly label it 'experimental', not only because Messiaen had already written a short passage of total birdsong in the fourth movement of *Messe de la Pentecôte*, but because it does not sound experimental, at least not when well played. But just as the strictly determined principles in the four *Études de rythme* were more acceptable when blended with freer ones in the following organ works, so the 'style oiseau' comes over with greater impact in *Oiseaux exotiques* (1956). There are many reasons for this. It is a shorter work than its predecessor, the alternation of sound-blocks is more frequent, and there are more long notes to anchor the attention, particularly on the brass and in the Greek and Hindu rhythms with which the percussion is almost exclusively concerned. Perhaps more than in any of these, the attraction of the work lies in the more imaginative, harmonically coloured piano writing. The change in the two years since *Réveil des oiseaux* is shown by Ex. 33, which contains (a) the opening of *Réveil* (b) the first cadenza of *Oiseaux exotiques*. The use of bass textures is very welcome

Ex. 33(a)

57

Ex. 33(b)

as a relief from the 'literal' interpretations of birdsong in the earlier work.

Of the changes in instrumentation the most noticeable are the addition of three gongs and the omission of strings. Messiaen explains the latter on practical grounds, that the strings tend to be drowned anyway in an orchestra of the size demanded by the later Romantic composers, or by Stravinsky in *Sacre du printemps*. But the orchestra in *Oiseaux exotiques* is small and a more cogent reason might be that strings are just not very good at imitating birds—however, see *Chronochromie*! The combination of wind, brass, and percussion produces a luminous sound in which the opposition of the birds to the rhythmic schemes of the percussion is plainly audible; it might even be argued that the sonority is an orchestral version of that in *Livre d'orgue*, where Messiaen denies himself the atmosphere of gamba and voix céleste so affectionately handled in all his earlier works for organ. A final reason for the piece's impact is the composer's structural use of the almost tonal call of the Indian white-rumped shama towards the end of the score (Ex. 34). With

Ex. 34

or without the pendant of the second bar, this call returns a further six times, in groups of two and finally four. The E major outline, the relatively square rhythm, and the Stravinskian spacing of the first chord all mark it as something out of the ordinary. After its final appearance the solo piano replies with the songs of two North American birds it has already played earlier (see min. sc. pp. 5–13). The orchestra, with piano, then lends its weight to this rebuttal of the shama theme with two calls from the very opening passage (bar 1, and 10–12 expanded); and, to obliterate all memories of interloping E major, the final chord, containing all twelve notes and spread over 6½ octaves, is repeated 31 times. The structural necessity for these repetitions is excuse enough but they are also a bird-call, of the white-crested laughing thrush whose 'implacable bursts of sound suggest some mountain giant'. So Messiaen contrives to be true both to his claim of faithfulness and to his instinct as a composer, a reconciliation that was vital to his next work, *Catalogue d'oiseaux* (1956–8).

This set of 13 piano pieces, lasting altogether a little under 2½ hours, can obviously not be treated in detail here, but generally there is a broadening of vocabulary. In places the chromatic modes return as do major and minor triads, either as a pedal over which birdsong develops or as the symbol of a natural phenomenon; for instance, the blue sea ('Le Merle bleu') is portrayed by mode II and dawn ('La Rousserolle effarvatte') by a combination of modes II, III, IV, and VI. In 'Le Loriot' also there is a passage of successive major 9ths that might almost be from a work by Debussy. As a contrast Ex. 35a, the open-

Ex. 35(a)

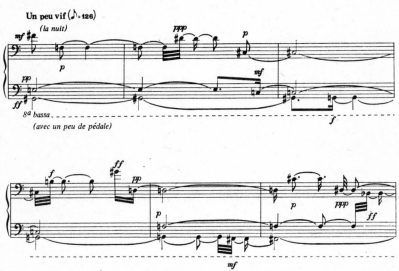

ing of 'La Chouette hulotte', could hardly have been written before 1950. It represents another and stricter attempt to embody the principles of *Mode de valeurs*, that is a unique correspondence of pitch, duration, and dynamics—Messiaen abandons the serialization of attacks which presents a formidable problem to any human performer. The three overlapping series of *Mode de valeurs* are here integrated into one, of great simplicity. The A♮ above middle C is given a duration of 1 demisemiquaver and descending continuously from it each note is 1 demisemiquaver longer than its predecessor, down to the bottom A♮ of the piano which has a duration of 49 demisemiquavers. This is a stricter application of the acoustical principles outlined in *Mode de valeurs*. The dynamics are arranged on a symmetrical plan of 7 levels, from A♮(*fff*) to D♯ (*ppp*) and down to the next A♮ (*fff*). As in *Mode*, Messiaen keeps for himself all decisions about which note comes next, for which he considers harmonic, textural, and dynamic criteria, but melody is hardly a relevant factor in an atmospheric passage entitled 'la nuit'. Here we see him, as at the end of *Oiseaux exotiques*, neatly combining art with science. The form of the piece is ABA'B', in which the second sections are merely extensions of the first; but it would be a mistake to imagine that Messiaen can be impressive only when he is doing something complex—Ex. 35b, the last 7 bars, shows what he can make out of two notes, C♮ and A♮.

Ex. 35(b)

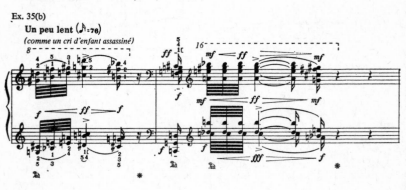

60

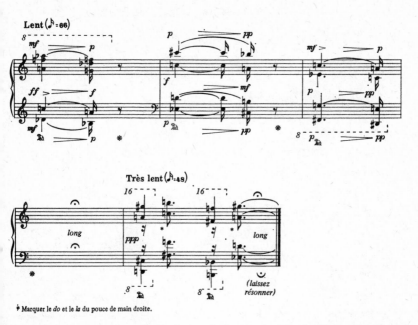

✦ Marquer le *do* et le *la* du pouce de main droite.

With the inspiring limitations of the piano in mind Messiaen has made the bird dialogues even sharper than in *Oiseaux exotiques* and in some cases, as in Ex. 36, from 'Le Traquet rieur', tonality plays a part. The contrast between the two songs is fairly clear from their

Ex. 36

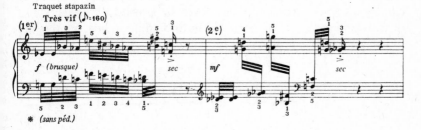

different speeds and textures but Messiaen turns this confrontation into a constructive argument. The 'merle bleu' ends his first phrase in a thinly disguised A major, the 'traquet stapazin' replies in a heavily disguised G major; then A major even more clearly, finally answered by an undisguised B major, giving an open end to the dialogue (readers, as the saying goes, may like to know that the piece ends in A major).

From this point we can trace a growing eclecticism in Messiaen's output. Not in the sense that he was to borrow ideas from other composers but that, so far, he has never again focused his attention so narrowly on just one of his own. The birds continue to sing, but they are no longer the onlie begetters of his music.

1960–1971

MESSIAEN's return to earlier interests is marked by the title and contents of his next work, *Chronochromie* (1960) for full orchestra. Heinrich Strobel in commissioning it was moved to insist: 'Attention, Messiaen! Cette-fois-ci, pas d'onde, pas de piano!' and so the piano is absent for the first time in one of his orchestral pieces since *L'Ascension* nearly 30 years before. We might therefore expect him, deprived of Loriod's percussive pianism, to move back towards the devotional, melodic style of that earlier work, but nothing of the sort occurs. Not only is the harmonic language grittier than ever but melody in the sense of a 'good tune' is quite absent; the nearest that Messiaen comes to it is in the corresponding movements 3 and 5 where he achieves an almost Schœnbergian intensity:

Ex. 37

The title means 'the colour of time' and the composer indicates that 'colour serves to make clear the temporal organization (les découpages du temps)'. But even though the colour is for him only a secondary consideration it is certainly what strikes the listener most forcibly at first hearing—a similar situation to that we have found already in *La Nativité* and *Turangalîla*. The strings, following their exclusion from *Oiseaux exotiques*, return, but very much as juniors in the orchestral partnership. Either they play extended trills and held chords as a background to the activity of woodwind and percussion, or perhaps they are allowed a brief moment of glory in depicting a mountain torrent; for long periods they are silent, and as if to compensate for this they are given the sixth movement to themselves—of which more below.

The work is in seven sections and the 'découpage du temps' extends to a strict measurement of the pauses between them. In inspiration the form, like the title, is Greek, from that of the chorus to a classical tragedy: an introduction leads to Strophe I, answered by Antistrophe I, Strophe II answered by Antistrophe II, Epôde, and a coda which refers back to the introduction. It must be said that the way Messiaen uses these forms bears little resemblance to their function in Greek drama, where each strophe had a strict rhythmic correspondence with its anti-strophe and where the introduction and coda, if any, would link the chorus to the action of the play and so relate only fortuitously to each other. In *Chronochromie* strophe relates not to antistrophe but to the other strophe. In other words Messiaen has found and adapted a form suitable to the mosaic construction he has always favoured.

For the strophes and for limited passages inside the other movements except the Epôde, the rhythmic organization is more complex, being based on the scheme which he calls 'interversions symmetriques', a development of the idea he had already tried out in *Île de feu II* and *Messe de la Pentecôte* (see Ex. 29). In general he first chooses an arbitrary order of note lengths, such as the following in units of a semi-quaver: 5, 4, 2, 8, 3, 1, 6, 7. He then takes each number as referring to the position inside the first 'interversion', the initial 5 to the fifth number (3), 4 to the fourth number (8), producing a second 'interversion': 3, 8, 4, 7, 2, 5, 1, 6—and so on. In *Chronochromie* he takes a larger series of 32 note values, giving him 36 possible interversions, and then deploys these interversions both singly and in simultaneous groups of 3. Each strophe is built over one complete version of 3 simultaneous groups, Strophe I over interversions 1, 2, 3, Strophe II over 22, 23, 24. The one obvious result of this is to make both strophes the same length; 33 bars of ⅜ followed by a shorter bar of silence. Messiaen entrusts these interversions to strings and percussion, each of the 3 groups being coloured not only by different percussion instruments but also by different types of chord on the strings. The pitch levels of the 3 groups are roughly an octave apart from each other but, as in *Mode de valeurs*, they overlap continually so that the impression is of a disturbed but continuous stream of thick, quiet chords. Over these, woodwind, glockenspiel, and xylophone play the songs of eight French birds in a free counterpoint of up to twelve parts; a development of the process in the 'Sortie' of *Messe de la Pentecôte* (Ex. 30). In the words of Antoine Goléa, Messiaen 'laisse, dans sa "Chronochromie", persister la féconde opposition entre la loi et la liberté' and, further, allows himself freedom in interpreting the laws of his own making. For instance, he uses only 16 of the 36 possible 'interversions' of the series, since 18 of the permutations are almost identical to the other 18. Paradoxically, then, even the strictness of the 'interversion' system is employed to create an apparent absence of system, or as the composer puts it, 'it is necessary to make a selection . . . in a way that will give the maximum opportunity for dissimilarity between one permutation and another.' This dissimilarity ensures that superimposed 'interversions' to an extent complement each other, in accordance with the traditional exigencies of counterpoint, but to the ear of the average listener the effect is random.

At the first performance, at Donaueschingen in 1960, the audience took exception to the sixth movement, 'Epôde'. It is an extension of the total birdsong of *Réveil des oiseaux*: 12 violins, 4 violas, and 2 cellos 'sing' the songs of birds in 18 real parts and there is only one abrupt change of texture in the nearly 4 minutes of hectic activity. The burden of their complaint was the movement's monotony and many critics in the following years have agreed with them, questioning Messiaen's attempt to impersonate birds by string instruments. But in his note on the first page of the Epôde the composer has already answered them: 'it is vital to avoid giving the impression of inextricable confusion at a single dynamic level. Certain birds must burst suddenly into the daylight and then return into the shadows.' Anyone lucky enough to have heard a performance given according to these instructions may well agree with the composer's retort to this movement's earliest detractors, 'Comme c'est drôle! Ils ont protesté contre le passage le plus gentil!' At all events, even the most sceptical must surely revel in the colour that comes flooding back in the first bars of the coda, and in the dramatic opposition of sounding brass to tinkling glockenspiel which marks a new 'rapprochement' between the worlds of *Turangalîla* and *Oiseaux exotiques*:

Ex. 38

How much the bolder gestures and more varied colours in *Chrono-chromie* owe to the piano's absence is hard to say. But in *Sept Haikai*, (1962) for piano and small orchestra, Messiaen returns us to a more intellectual milieu. Greek and Hindu rhythms, rhythmic canons, and melismata of terrifying virtuosity combine to create a highly individual atmosphere, unemotional, mysterious, yet catching something of Japanese precision and delicacy. The piano performs cadenzas or forms an ensemble with xylophone and marimba, as in *Oiseaux exotiques*, but now there is a clear difference between its styles in these two activities. The cadenzas continue to employ the 'style oiseau' with its well-articulated sections and internal repeats, while in general the percussion ensemble demands of the piano a succession of textures that are abstract to the point of incoherence, when viewed out of context. The piano's definitive contribution to the work as a whole becomes clear when we look at its structure. Movements I, VII (introduction and coda) corresponding material, piano abstract; II, V evocations of place, piano abstract (even though in V it plays only three chords over and over again); III, VI evocations of place with birds, 'style oiseau' involving almost identical birds, piano in cadenzas only (III) or continuing the cadenza style into the ensemble (VI); IV imitation of Japanese music, no piano. This careful grading emphasizes the emotional flux of the piece, a crescendo to the centre balanced by a decrescendo to the original level. The sharp, concise cadenzas of III whet the listener's appetite for the eventual emergence of a tune in the central 'Gagaku', a recreation of the ceremonial music of the imperial Japanese court in which Messiaen imitates the 'hichiriki', a primitive oboe, by combining two modern oboes with cor anglais and trumpet in unison. From this melodic climax there is a gradual descent, through the less dominating brass theme of V, the harsh call of the 'uguisu' and the piano cadenzas of VI, to the ultimate, that is the initial, contemplative calm of the coda.

66

Apart from its great intrinsic beauty, 'Gagaku' is important in Messiaen's development because it was the first melodically based music he had written for over 10 years. In the explorations of timbre and rhythm, melody had, it seemed, been forgotten. If the imperial Japanese court is not necessarily the environment from which we would expect a revival to come, *gagaku* had the obvious advantage of being, in the best sense, exotic; that is, free of the outmoded associations which almost any Western melody was bound to excite. 'Almost', because another source, plainsong, was lying where Messiaen had left it after *Vingt Regards*. Between these melodic forms of East and West there is a bond, of dignity and of respect for the individual note which is treasured and savoured before being gently and gracefully abandoned:

Ex. 39 (a)

Ex. 39 (b)

67

Couleurs de la cité céleste (1963), like *Chronochromie*, was commissioned by Heinrich Strobel, but this time Messiaen found himself unable to compose strictly inside the proposed limitations—of 3 trombones and 3 xylophones! However, the opposition of rich, sustained brass chords to high, furious fusillades from the percussion is retained in the ampler scoring he allowed himself. Apart from one short organ piece, *Verset pour la fête de la Dédicace* (1960), this was the first work of specifically Christian inspiration that he had written for 12 years. It is based on five quotations from the Apocalypse to which he was led by the apocalyptic nature of the trombone's sound, and from the store of plainsong he has chosen four alleluias, treating them in both a free and strict manner. Ex. 39b is a straightforward enunciation of the Alleluia for Corpus Christi, set over Messiaen's individual brand of harmony. At other times the alleluias are preserved only in outline with the melodic intervals changed and at three places a version of the Alleluia for the 4th Sunday after Easter is treated as a 'mélodie de timbres', à la Webern.

Plainsong apart, there are ostensibly no other features in *Couleurs* that call for comment—Messiaen himself calls it a compendium of his previous techniques—but the plainsong has its effect on the material round it. Texturally, in its capacity as melody it tends to reduce the 'style oiseau' once more to the level of decoration; at the same time its relative slowness is mirrored in the increasing proportion of chordal writing, even where an alleluia is not itself the melodic basis. As the form of the work is a typical mosaic, only one of the nearly 50 sections being longer than a minute, the wider variety of tempo is very welcome to the ear. The quasi-tonal alleluias also have a harmonic influence in spite of Ex. 39b, even though no triads make an appearance unalloyed. At fig. 75 in Ex. 40, mode II is presented directly, after some five years of

Ex. 40

disuse. The dramatic conflict of Ex. 39b is now superficially resolved and only the stubborn refusal of the piano to bring its rhythms into line belies this resolution.

The harmonic scheme of this passage is worth looking at. Bars 1–3 use all 12 notes of the scale; in 4–6 C♮ is missing; and in the remaining phrases the notes are further reduced to 9 or 8, giving in fact three different modes in succession (II, III, IV). This gradual refining of the harmonies into a modal individuality gives a sense of movement to these apparently solid blocks of sound.

Whether or not the alleviation by plainsong of the 'style oiseau' makes things easier for the listener, Messiaen does seem to have achieved a more subtle integration of diverse elements in this work than in *Sept Haikai*. The birdsongs too are more individual—the screeching Araponga, the menacing Arapaçu, and the Stournelle whose limpid notes twice calm the storms of brass and tam-tam (Ex. 41). Messiaen

Ex. 41

introduces the piano cadenzas more sparingly now and is firmer in controlling the birds' volubility. Before the statement of the Alleluia for Corpus Christi which concludes the work, he repeats the effect—not the details—of Ex. 42, and this reference across some two-thirds of the piece is worth a deal of persistent avian jubilation.

What is often called Messiaen's 'monumental' style can be traced back as far at least as *Livre d'orgue* (Ex. 32) through *Chronochromie* to *Couleurs*, although operating here at an unobtrusive level. It now received external encouragement with the commission from André Malraux for a work to commemorate the dead of two World Wars.

Et exspecto resurrectionem mortuorum (1964) was given its first performance in the Sainte Chapelle, whose wonderful windows made their
contribution to the colourful resonances of Messiaen's orchestra, and
he had composed it with spacious acoustics in mind. The overwhelming
impression is of a new grandeur and simplicity, symbolized by the
ascent from the initial low A♭ on the saxhorn to the final piccolo G♯
five octaves higher. For the first time both piano and strings are
excluded from the orchestra, as are the three 'xylos' which figured so
largely in *Couleurs*. Instead of their brittle hysteria, a hieratic solemnity
invests the proceedings, deepened by mysterious strokes on gongs and
tam-tams and by huge, dissonant chords from woodwind and brass.

The correspondence of material between outer movements is still
close, as it was between introduction and coda in both *Chronochromie*
and *Sept Haikai*, but Messiaen now reinforces this with subtler links
as well, even though the sections themselves are longer than in *Couleurs*
and the listener has ample time to acclimatize himself. For example,
the 'de profundis' theme of the first movement reappears, as we shall
see, in the fourth; both third and fourth movements include ritual
strokes on percussion as structural elements; and the tritone is a feature
in the melodies of all movements—the very fact that we can use the
word 'melody' indicates the importance of 'Gagaku' in *Sept Haikai*.

The first of the five movements, 'De profundis . . .', ends (Ex. 42)

Ex. 42

with eight chords evoking the 'cry of the abyss' (see Ex. 31) and they afford a fascinating parallel with the harmonic thinking we have already observed behind Ex. 40. Each of the eight chord-pairs contains all twelve notes, split between its two levels. The first four chord-pairs are arranged in an ABA′B′ pattern, but although the harmonies correspond between themselves they do not belong to any recognized aggregation of notes. With the fifth chord this anarchy is set in order, the first chord of each pair being made up from 7 of the 9 notes of mode III, the second of the pair filling in the remaining 5 notes. The feeling of resolution is unmistakable as the exact shape of the fifth chord is not reproduced until the last one. Thus the whole example is constructed as ABA′B′CDEC′ and unified further by the simple outline of the trumpet melody.

In the second movement Messiaen harks back to the clarinet solo in *Quatuor pour la fin du temps*, but before we hear the tune as such he prefigures it with two disguised versions, as arabesque and as harmony:

Ex. 43

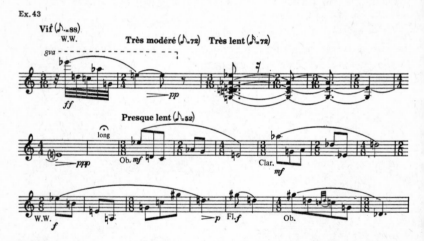

Of these three aspects of the truth, the melody is the only one that can be made to unfold its secrets at length. It is the release for the tension built up by the arabesque and the chord and is therefore impelled well beyond the original six-note motif into a long thread of sound, characterized by the ubiquitous tritone. The second limb of the melody (bars 12–14) forms the basis of another correspondence that binds together the whole movement, whose last paragraph treats these bars in the same way—as arabesque, harmony, and melody.

So far there have been no birds, and indeed they might seem

inappropriate to such a sombre undertaking. Messiaen however finds not only a musical but an intellectual justification for including in the third movement the song of the Amazonian Uirapuru. Formally this movement is extremely simple, an almost identical two-fold repetition of four distinct timbres and materials: Uirapuru, bells, general crescendo, low brass with woodwind merging into tam-tam and gongs. Of these four only the birdsong has any improvisatory feel about it. The rest stay within the monumental style (and in the case of the brass passage within the melodic influence) of the opening movement, and they are all the more impressive for the contrast with the unformalized birdsong that precedes them. One can go further and say that without the bird-song they would have no point. Already with the second solo of the Uirapuru we are expecting the inevitable and Messiaen surprises only by a minute lengthening of the crescendo section. By limiting himself to one bird, represented in a relatively slow, chordal, non-contrapuntal manner, he brings the 'style oiseau' into a closer relationship with adjacent material and at the same time increases its potential as a source of energy. Musically, then, there can be little doubt that the Uirapuru is a success, but why is it here at all in a movement entitled 'The hour comes when the dead shall hear the voice of the Son of God'? Because it is a bird 'that one hears, apparently, on one's deathbed and which symbolizes here that inner voice which will be the voice of Christ summoning the dead from their sleep and indicating that the resurrection is at hand'.

In the fourth movement strokes on the tam-tam introduce alternately passages of modified plainsong (Introit and Alleluia for Easter Sunday) and the song of the Calandra Lark 'symbolizing heavenly joy and one of the four qualities of the Heavenly Host, the "gift of agility"'. The overall plan is such a striking example of the complexity without complication which Dukas enjoined on his pupil that it deserves to be presented in detail:

Tam-tam *pp*/ plainsong (22 bars)/ tam-tam *p*/ lark (37) //
tam-tam *f*/ plainsong (27)/ tam-tam *ff* / lark (45) //
tam-tam *fff*/ plainsong 'de profundis' (44)/ tam-tam gongs *p,f*/ 8 long chords

Within the rigidity of this plan the increasing length of the plainsong and lark passages and the increasing dynamics of the tam-tam strokes prepare for the explosion of the 'de profundis' theme from the first movement . . . and there many a composer would have ended; no further volume can safely be extracted from the tam-tams, no further combination of themes could cap the climax already achieved. Instead

Messiaen presents a resumé of the overall crescendo of the movement in the piano/forte strokes of the tam-tam. He mingles this with the fresh sonority of gongs so that we are at once satisfied with the resumé and prepared for some new, conclusive idea. Eight massive chords recall the eight that ended the first movement (Ex. 42).

The fifth and last movement is hewn out of one block of stone. 'The sound of a great multitude' rises and falls in a measured pulsing until the rhythmic mould breaks, to release a flood of dissonant chords that achieve their long-awaited goal in what is effectively a D♭ major triad.

Over four years passed after the first performance of *Et exspecto* until Messiaen brought a new work before the public. In response to a commission from the Gulbenkian Foundation, he wrote his largest orchestral work to date, *La Transfiguration de Notre Seigneur Jésus-Christ* (1963–9). Space prevents any detailed discussion of this meditation on different aspects of the mystery of the Transfiguration of Christ, but a few general points may be mentioned. As in *Et exspecto* a rigid formal plan serves as a foil to the imaginative contents. The 14 movements are divided into two 'septenaries'. Each septenary is further divided into two sections consisting of a gospel narrative and two meditations, and completed by a chorale. The 'monumental' style is still fully in evidence but, perhaps partly in deference to the limitations of the chorus, the harmonic language shows a retreat from the starkness of *Et exspecto* and includes now the unashamed glory of pure major triads, E major replacing the F♯ major of former years. At the other end of the sensory scale, birds, Greek and Hindu rhythms, recitatives in the manner of plainsong (in which the tritone is again prominent), and chords of a mountainous dissonance find their place in this celebration of the light of Christ's glory that 'hath shone anew upon the eyes of our mind'. Beyond the ambit of these formulae lie the moments of sheer imaginative genius, such as the extraordinary metallic eruption that greets the cry 'Gloria in excelsis Deo'.

In 1970 he wrote a pendant to the *Catalogue d'oiseaux*, *La Fauvette des jardins*, which in its harmonies and use of the piano conforms closely with the earlier collection. His most recent major work is the *Méditations sur le mystère de la Sainte-Trinité* (1969) which, like *La Trans-figuration*, forms a synthesis, and for us a more convenient one, of nearly all his previous techniques. But before looking at this aspect we should first discuss the one quite new element in the work, what Messiaen calls the 'communicable language'. He has formed this by assigning a definite pitch and duration to each letter, beginning with the natural pitches for A–H but extending this musical alphabet by arranging the letters according to their sonic groups, as linguals, sibilants etc. With this language he then expresses in music three quotations from the *Summa* of St. Thomas Aquinas, from whom he had also taken a number of texts for *La Transfiguration*. Linguistic details are really not of great importance to anyone but the composer. Much more interesting is why he thought the language necessary in the first place; he invented it 'as a game and to renew my thought'. In other words, it plays precisely the same part in his music as the song of the blackcap, the rhythm râgavardhana, or the Alleluia for Easter Day in providing a challenge to his technique, a springboard for his imagination. As Stravinsky wrote in *Poetics of Music*: 'My freedom will be so much the greater and more meaningful the more narrowly I limit my field of action and the more I surround myself with obstacles.'

As an example we may take the beginning of the third movement, in which the right hand is entirely built from the communicable language, on the text: 'La relation réelle en Dieu est réellement identique à l'essence.' Of this Messiaen keeps only nouns, verbs, and some adjectives—'relation . . . (en) Dieu est . . . identique (à) essence . . .'—and reproduces the pronouns in brackets by set formulae in the manner of the Latin case system (Ex. 44). Meanwhile left hand and pedal expound

Ex. 44

R. bombarde 16', trp. 8', clairon 4', | P. et G. fonds 16', 8', 4', – P.G.— | Péd. fonds 16', 8', sb. 32'–
et tous les fonds 16', 8', 4',– ⤐ | (sans les montres et sans les prestants) | tir P. et G.|

various Hindu rhythms, the left hand continuously, the pedal separated by freely placed silences. In the last four bars of our example the right hand plays the 'theme of God', like the one in *Vingt Regards* (Ex. 20) a unifying factor in the whole work. If the two themes, with nearly 30 years between them, sound very different, this does not deny their structural identity as leitmotifs; Messiaen refers to Wagner's term in describing the above 9-note phrase.

But his most amazing achievement in the *Méditations* is the synthesis we mentioned earlier. The materials he incorporates go back beyond his own earlier styles to include a diatonic language that we find in Debussy or the 'classical' Stravinsky. He also re-embraces timbres like that of gamba and voix céleste. But nearly all the discoveries of his middle years also, together with the communicable language, are somehow brought into harmony with this older generation of sound.

Finally, let us admire the intellectual control that Messiaen continues to exert over the outpourings of his heart. The song of the Yellowhammer, for instance, is not squandered but carefully reserved as a seal to be set on four of the work's nine movements. Even its cumulative influence on these four (II, V, VIII, IX) is not taken for granted but reinforced by discreet rhythmic or melodic preparations. The apparently effortless sequence of ideas, the extraordinary oneness of emotion between diatonic and chromatic passages, and the reckless handling of explosive clichés are nowhere better demonstrated than at the end of the eighth movement, where everything springs from the Alleluia's last five notes:

Ex. 45

(Bruant jaune)

ENVOI

WHETHER the communicable language will lead Messiaen along new paths to territory where there is neither bird, nor plainsong, nor chromatic mode, we must wait and see. It seems likely, on the basis of his development so far, that even if this does happen he would eventually return to a style in which some at least of these techniques were again compounded, to the discomfort of those who are still worried by his use of such diverse and complex means. But his open mind is an essential part of his character, and in our narrowly specialist age we should derive some comfort from the image of the French composer conversing in Latin with a Japanese ornithologist. This innate receptivity is one reason for his outstanding success as a teacher and, as he does not make slaves of his pupils, neither does he allow himself to be the slave of any of his techniques. When so many French composers in the last 100 years have been intrigued by the rhythms of Spain, why should he not be by those of ancient Greece and India? Of all his interests, he has a 'secret preference' for rhythm, recognizing modestly his own contribution in getting composers of the mid-20th century to think again about this neglected element of music. The *Traité de rythme*, on which he has long been at work, is the only promise he has made about what we may expect from him in the years to come—for the rest, he prefers to quote a Chinese proverb: 'The future is dark as a lake.'

SELECT BIBLIOGRAPHY

EVERY student should start from Messiaen's own *Technique de mon langage musical* (2 vols, Paris, 1944) available in a good English, that is to say American, translation: a thorough survey of the ingredients in his style up to and including *Visions de l'Amen*. Robert Sherlaw Johnson's *Messiaen* will be published very shortly. Other sources in English, apart from dictionary articles, are David Drew's 'Messiaen—A Provisional Study' (*The Score*, Dec. 1954, Sept., Dec. 1955), his, more accessible, contribution to the symposium *European Music in the Twentieth Century* (London, 1961, ed. Hartog) and Stuart Waumsley's short volume *The Organ Music of Olivier Messiaen* (Paris, 1968).

In French, Claude Rostand's *Olivier Messiaen* (Paris, 1957) and especially Antoine Goléa's *Rencontres avec Olivier Messiaen* (Paris, 1960) are well worth reading. Two more recent books by younger authors are *Olivier Messiaen* by Pierrette Mari (Paris, 1965) and *Entretiens avec Olivier Messiaen* by Claude Samuel (Paris, 1967), in the second of which the composer's reticence is almost wholly dispersed by the tact and expertise of his interviewer.